Simple and Delicious
BARBECUE

Vicki Liley

APPLE

34 / 371

Contents

Introducing Barbecues

Barbecuing is one of the oldest and simplest forms of cooking. It has been a way of life for decades. A barbecue creates an atmosphere with its tantalizing smells and intense flavors of the food—hot, sweet, salty and bitter—made using an array of fresh meats, fruits and vegetables.

Having a barbecue is a perfect way to enjoy some casual al fresco dining with a gathering of friends or family. Outdoor barbecues lend themselves to garden entertaining areas where people can gather while the meal is cooking and enjoy the sunshine or balmy evening breezes. But if the weather or space doesn't permit outdoor cooking and dining, an indoor grill, or even a simple stove-top grill pan, can still provide a unique way of cooking food with friends.

Over the years barbecuing has come to incorporate the flavors and cooking traditions of many different countries. The delicious and simple recipes featured in this book are inspired from cultures all around the world—from Asia to the Mediterranean. Many of the recipes use marinades, rubs or flavored butters to enhance the flavor of the meat, fish or vegetables and in some cases even improve it. With a good soaking in olive oil and a mixture of your favorite herbs and spices, a cheaper cut of meat or piece of fish can be transformed from the ordinary into something extraordinary.

The choice of the type of barbecue you use will depend on several things, including the number of people you will entertain, the location of the barbecue, storage and the size of the cooking area needed. For example, if the cooking area is too small, the grill will become congested and food won't cook properly. It will also depend on whether you prefer the quick convenience of a gas barbecue that lights automatically, or the challenge of starting a fire with a charcoal grill. Select a model and type that suits your needs.

Armed with the right barbecue, the proper utensils and the delicious recipes featured in this book, your next barbecue is sure to be a great success.

Equipment

There are many types of barbecues and pans available. Outdoor and indoor grilling is essentially the same, but outdoor barbecues lend themselves to garden entertaining areas where friends and family can gather while the meal is cooking. Indoor grilling can be done on a tabletop with a Japanese-style hibachi or electric countertop grill, or in a stove-top grill pan in the kitchen.

Most of the recipes in this book generally require only a small grill or barbecue. The Japanese-style hibachi is ideal: compact, portable and inexpensive, it is suitable for small balconies and for either indoor or outdoor cooking. It uses charcoal for its heat source.

ABOVE *Charcoal barbecue*

ABOVE *Gas kettle barbecue (left); standard charcoal barbecue (right)*

The modern electric countertop grill has a nonstick surface, generally has three or more heat settings, and can be opened flat for a larger cooking surface. Chargrill pans are available in cast iron or nonstick aluminum and are used on gas or electric stove tops. They are easy to clean and store, and are ideal for everyday cooking for up to six people. A well-ventilated kitchen or exhaust hood is recommended.

The easy-to-use barbecue has multiple heat settings and is available in many sizes and models in all price ranges. Some are connected to a home's gas supply, while others use portable gas bottles or tanks.

Disposable barbecues that use presoaked charcoal briquettes are inexpensive and require no messy clean-up. They must be used on a heatproof rock or brick base and disposed of carefully.

Light-weight portable barbecues, generally heated with charcoal or wood chips, are simply a smaller version of the home barbecue and are ideal for grilling anywhere.

Kettle barbecues, heated by charcoal or gas, are available in various lidded sizes, from small to very large. The closed lid allows the heated air to rise and circulate around the food in a manner similar to a convection oven. This makes it ideal for roasting meat and poultry as well as the more common steaks and sausages.

ABOVE *Charcoal kettle barbecue*

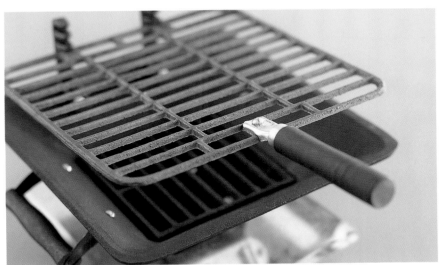

TOP Stove-top grill (ridged grill) pan
ABOVE Hibachi grill

Utensils

Long-handled utensils, like tongs, forks and metal spatulas, are essential for turning foods during cooking. A serrated spatula can also be useful. Keep a separate pair of long-handled tongs for moving coals around if need be. Heatproof mitts are also essential, and basting brushes and an apron may come in handy.

Grilled food on skewers has an attractive appeal to cooks and diners alike because of the different flavors, textures and colors that can be cooked and served as one unit. Threading combinations of food onto skewers can also make small quantities of expensive ingredients go a long way.

The foods threaded onto skewers should have the same cooking time, or longer-cooking foods such as potato should be parboiled beforehand. Bamboo skewers need soaking in water for 10 minutes before any food is threaded onto them to prevent them from burning.

Both bamboo and stainless steel skewers are available in many sizes. Select the size best suited for the food and the occasion. For example, small cubes of chicken for a party are best threaded onto small bamboo skewers so guests can dispose of the skewers after eating. Stainless steel skewers require cleaning after each use.

Fresh rosemary and bay leaf stems can be used as an attractive and flavorsome alternative to bamboo or stainless steel skewers. However, make sure the stems are woody, not the young soft stems, and soak them in water before use. Lemongrass, sugarcane and bamboo shoots are also sometimes used as skewers for grilling food.

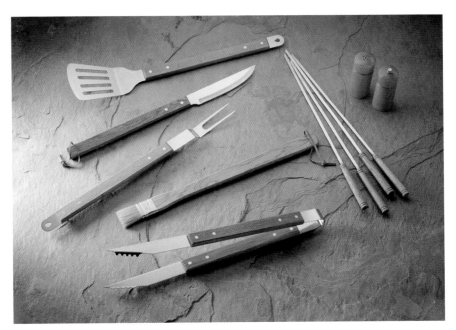

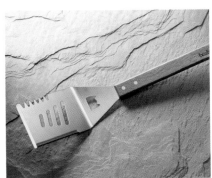

TOP (anticlockwise from top) Long-handled spatula, knife, fork, basting brush, tongs, stainless steel skewers; salt and pepper shakers ABOVE Heatproof mitts (left); serrated spatula (right)

Getting started

Starting a gas grill is easy. Open the lid and make sure the burner controls are off and there is fuel in the tank or bottle. Turn on the fuel and light according to manufacturer's instructions. Preheat on high for 10 minutes before cooking.

If using a charcoal grill, charcoal briquettes are easy to use. The most common way to start a charcoal fire is to build a pyramid of charcoal on a grate in the fire pan, soak it with the lighter fluid if the briquettes aren't presoaked and light it carefully. Alternatively, 4 or 5 firelighters can be inserted throughout the charcoal and lit with a taper or long safety match. Use only barbecue firelighters, as those designed for domestic fires contain paraffin which can spoil the food. After about 25 minutes, the coals should be lit properly. The coals can then be rearranged and the grate or barbecue plate placed over the top.

A popular and ecological alternative to using lighter fluid or presoaked briquettes is the charcoal chimney starter, a sheet metal cylinder, available at barbecue outlets. Place the chimney starter on the grate, stuff crumpled newspaper in the base, pile charcoal briquettes on top and light the paper. The coals are ready when covered with pale grey ash, generally in about 20 minutes. Carefully distribute the coals over the grate.

For electric countertop grills, plug into the power source, turn on and preheat according to the manufacturer's instructions. For stove-top chargrill pans, place the clean pan over high heat on the stove and preheat for 5 minutes before cooking. For disposable barbecues, follow the manufacturer's instructions.

Controlling the heat

Heat is regulated in a charcoal grill by moving the briquettes with a set of long-handled tongs. Push them closer together to intensify the heat, or spread them apart to cool down the fire. The air vents on a barbecue provide a similar control. Open them to increase the heat, or close them to decrease it. On a gas barbecue, the control dials make it easy to regulate the heat. If flames flare up on a gas barbecue, don't spray with water. The steam can cause burns and can sometimes crack the enamel finish on your barbecue. Instead, close the lid and close the air vents.

Cleaning

Follow the manufacturer's instructions for cleaning gas, charcoal and other barbecues. To clean the cooking grill of a gas barbecue, turn the burners to high, close the lid and allow to heat for 5 minutes. Then use a long-handled wire brush to scrape off any food residue. When the grill cools, remove it and clean with hot soapy water. Keep the bottom tray and the grease-catch pan clean to prevent fires.

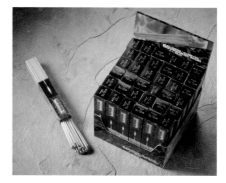

ABOVE (clockwise from top left) Gas lighter; long safety matches; wire cleaning brush; firelighters

Step-by-step Guide

Flavored butters

A slice of flavored butter placed onto a hot-from-the-grill piece of fish, chicken, meat or vegetable forms a warm buttery sauce. Flavored butters are a quick and tasty means of providing additional seasonings. Butters can be made up to 3–4 days ahead of time or frozen for up to 2 months. Flavored butters are rolled into logs, then sliced, scooped or piped onto cooked foods. They are also a delicious spread for warm grilled bread.

For 1 lb (500 g) fish or seafood
OPTION 1
4 oz (125 g) softened butter
grated rind and juice of 1 lime
OPTION 2
4 oz (125 g) softened butter
2 tablespoons chopped fresh cilantro
   (coriander) leaves
1 tablespoon chopped chervil
1 clove garlic, chopped
juice of 1 lemon

For 1 lb (500 g) beef, lamb or pork
OPTION 1
4 oz (125 g) softened butter
2 teaspoons chopped rosemary
1 small red chili pepper, seeded and
   finely chopped
freshly ground black pepper

For 1 lb (500 g) beef, lamb or pork
OPTION 2
4 oz (125 g) softened butter
2 cloves garlic, chopped
2 scallions (shallots/spring onions),
   finely chopped
freshly ground black pepper

For 1 lb (500 g) chicken
OPTION 1
4 oz (125 g) softened butter
2 canned anchovy fillets, drained and
   mashed
juice of 1 lemon
freshly ground black pepper
OPTION 2
4 oz (125 g) softened butter
2 cloves garlic, finely chopped
1 small green chili pepper, seeded and
   finely chopped
grated rind and juice of 1 lime

1. Using a wooden spoon or an electric mixer, beat butter until soft.

2. Add flavorings and mix well.

3. Spoon onto a piece of plastic wrap and shape into a log.

4. Remove plastic wrap and slice into rounds to serve.

Dry coatings

Dry mixtures of breadcrumbs, herbs and spices add flavor and texture to barbecued food. They can also protect the food from the harsh heat of the grill, resulting in a more subtle, grilled flavor. A simple coating of breadcrumbs can keep food moist inside while creating a crisp and crunchy outside. Food coated in a blend of fresh herbs and spices can be left to marinate before cooking.

Dry coatings best suit thinner portions that cook quickly so the coatings don't burn. Partially cook longer-cooking foods before coating and grilling them.

For 2 fish fillets
grated rind of 1 lemon or 1 lime
2 tablespoons chopped fresh cilantro (coriander) leaves
1 tablespoon chopped chervil
sea salt and freshly ground black pepper to taste

For 4 chicken breast fillets
3 tablespoons fresh white breadcrumbs
1 small red chili pepper, seeds removed and chopped
2 tablespoons chopped basil leaves

grated rind of 1 lime
1 clove garlic, finely chopped
sea salt and freshly ground black pepper to taste

For 1 lb (500 g) beef, lamb or pork
1 teaspoon five spice powder
1 teaspoon sea salt
1 teaspoon freshly ground black pepper
2 tablespoons chopped fresh cilantro (coriander) leaves
1 small red chili pepper, seeded and chopped

1. Brush food with oil and coat in prepared coating mixture.

2. Cook on a preheated oiled grill or barbecue.

Marinades

One of the easiest ways to add flavor to food before grilling is to marinate. Foods can be marinated for a few minutes or up to several hours, and even overnight. The longer the marinating time, the stronger the flavor will be, so don't marinate delicately flavored foods like fish for too long—30 minutes is usually sufficient. At least 3 hours is recommended for marinating skinless chicken (12 hours with skin) and to really tenderize beef or lamb, 8 hours to overnight is ideal. Food should be refrigerated while marinating but brought back to room temperature before cooking to achieve optimum flavor.

Marinating enhances the moisture level of the food, keeping it juicy and more succulent after cooking. Leftover marinades can be brushed over the food while it is cooking, or heated and served as a sauce with the cooked meal, but make sure always to boil the marinade for at least 1 minute before serving.

Because many marinades have an acid-based ingredient, it is best to marinate food in shallow nonmetallic dishes. Heavy-duty plastic bags are also good for marinating foods.

Prepared marinades can be stored in screw-top jars in the refrigerator for up to two weeks.

Sweet chili marinade

For 1 lb/ (500 g) fish, seafood or chicken
2 tablespoons vegetable oil
2 tablespoons Thai sweet chili sauce
2 tablespoons lemon or lime juice
3 cloves garlic, chopped
3 teaspoons grated ginger
1 tablespoon chopped fresh cilantro
    (coriander) leaves
salt and pepper to taste

Thai lime marinade

For 2 lb (1 kg) shrimp (prawns), baby octopus or fish fillets
1 cup (8 fl oz/250 ml) coconut milk
¼ cup (2 fl oz/60 ml) olive oil
¼ cup (2 fl oz/60 ml) lime juice
2 tablespoons finely grated lime zest
1 tablespoon finely grated fresh ginger
2 cloves garlic, crushed
2 small red chili peppers, thinly sliced
2 tablespoons packed brown sugar
1 tablespoon fish sauce

Soy and basil marinade

For 1 lb (500 g) beef, lamb or pork
2 tablespoons vegetable oil
1 tablespoon chopped basil leaves
3 tablespoons soy sauce
grated rind of 1 lemon
3 cloves garlic, chopped
salt and pepper to taste

Sweet and sour marinade

For 3 lb (1½ kg) pork (spareribs, loin or chops)
1 small pineapple, peeled, cut
  lengthwise into quarters, cored and
  thinly sliced (or 1½ lb/750 g tinned
  pineapple)
½ cup (4 fl oz/60 ml) pineapple juice
¼ cup (2 fl oz/60 ml) lime juice
2 cloves crushed garlic
1 small red chili pepper, finely chopped
¼ cup (2 oz/60 g) packed brown sugar

Ginger marinade

For 1 lb/ (500 g) vegetables
2 tablespoons vegetable oil
2 teaspoons sesame oil
2 cloves garlic, chopped
2 teaspoons grated ginger
salt and pepper to taste

Grapefruit and brandy marinade

For 2¼ lb (1.1 kg) lamb
½ cup (4 fl oz/125 ml) grapefruit juice
1 grapefruit, peeled, pith removed, cut
  into segments and seeded
¼ cup (3 oz/90 g) honey
¼ cup (2 fl oz/60 ml) brandy
¼ cup (2 fl oz/60 ml) dry white wine
2 tablespoons fresh thyme leaves
freshly ground pepper

Cranberry marinade

For 2 lb (1 kg) poultry or fish
1½ cups (6½ oz/200 g) cranberries
2 tablespoons red wine vinegar
¼ cup (2 fl oz/60 ml) olive oil
2 tablespoons finely grated orange zest
2 cinnamon sticks
1 tablespoon finely grated fresh ginger
3 tablespoons packed brown sugar

Raspberry marinade

For 1½ lb (750 g) poultry or fish
1 cup (8 oz/250 g) raspberries
¼ cup (2 fl oz/60 ml) raspberry vinegar
½ cup (4 fl oz/125 ml) olive oil
¼ cup (⅓ oz/10 g) fresh tarragon
  leaves
freshly ground pepper

1. Place marinade ingredients in a screw-top jar or jug and mix well.

2. Place fish, chicken, meat or vegetables into a shallow non metallic dish.

3. Pour or brush marinade over food. Cover and refrigerate.

4. Drain, then cook on heated grill, basting regularly with leftover marinade.

Chicken

Skewered barbecued chicken

Serves 6

2 chickens, each about 2 lb (1 kg)
½ cup (4 fl oz/125 ml) lemon juice
1 large yellow (brown) onion, grated
2 teaspoons salt
freshly ground pepper
¼ cup (2 fl oz/60 ml) butter, melted
1 teaspoon paprika
cherry tomatoes, for garnish

Using poultry shears or a very sharp knife, cut each chicken in half lengthwise and remove backbone. Cut each half into six pieces that are nearly equal in size: halve breast pieces and thighs, chop off bony end of leg, and leave wing intact.

In a glass or ceramic bowl, combine lemon juice, onion, salt and pepper to taste. Add chicken pieces, turning in marinade to coat. Cover with plastic wrap and marinate for 3–4 hours in refrigerator, turning chicken occasionally.

Prepare barbecue, preferably with charcoal.

Thread chicken onto six long, flat metal skewers, placing the thicker pieces in the center, and packing all the pieces close together. In a small bowl, combine melted butter with paprika and brush over chicken. Place chicken on a grill (barbecue) rack, basting frequently with butter mixture and turning often, until chicken is cooked through, 15–20 minutes.

Remove chicken from skewers if desired and garnish with blistered cherry tomatoes.

To blister cherry tomatoes: Cut an X on the bottom of each tomato and thread onto skewers if necessary. Brush with melted butter and cook on grill (barbecue) rack until skin blisters and browns lightly.

Lime chicken and pork patties

Serves 4

1 lb (500 g) ground (minced) chicken thigh meat

8 oz (250 g) ground (minced) lean pork meat

8 scallions (shallots/spring onions), chopped

3 cloves garlic, finely chopped

3 small red chili peppers, one seeded and finely chopped, 2 seeded and sliced

¼ cup (⅓ oz/10 g) finely chopped fresh cilantro (coriander) leaves

2 teaspoons grated kaffir lime rind

2 tablespoons kaffir lime juice

1½ cups (3 oz/90 g) fresh white breadcrumbs

1 egg, beaten

2 tablespoons vegetable oil

12 fresh basil leaves

1 baby Romaine (cos) lettuce, leaves separated and washed, for serving

In a large mixing bowl, place chicken, pork, scallions, garlic, chopped chili pepper, cilantro, rind, juice, breadcrumbs and egg. Using wet hands, mix until well combined. Divide into 12 portions and shape each into a round patty. Place in a single layer on a plate, cover with plastic wrap and refrigerate for 1 hour.

Preheat a grill pan or barbecue, then brush grill lightly with oil. Grill patties until golden and tender, 2–3 minutes each side. Remove from grill. In a small saucepan, warm leftover vegetable oil and fry basil leaves and the 2 sliced chili peppers until aromatic, about 1 minute.

To serve, place chicken patties onto serving plates with lettuce leaves and top each with fried basil and chili peppers.

Spicy chicken skewers with mint yogurt

Serves 4
1 lb (500 g) chicken breast fillets
3 teaspoons ground coriander
2 teaspoons ground turmeric
1 small red chili pepper, seeded and finely chopped
4 cloves garlic, finely chopped
2 tablespoons superfine (caster) sugar
1 teaspoon sea salt
12 bamboo skewers
2 tablespoons peanut oil

6½ oz (200 g) choy sum or other Asian greens, coarsely chopped
MINT YOGURT
½ cup (4 fl oz/125 ml) plain (natural) yogurt
2 cloves garlic, finely chopped
2 tablespoons freshly chopped mint leaves
¼ cup (1½ oz/40 g) peeled, seeded and chopped cucumber

Cut chicken fillets into 1½-inch (4-cm) cubes. In a bowl, combine ground coriander, turmeric, chili pepper, garlic, sugar and salt and toss chicken pieces in spice mixture. Cover bowl with plastic wrap and refrigerate for 2 hours. Soak bamboo skewers in water for 10 minutes, then drain. Thread chicken pieces onto bamboo skewers. Preheat a grill pan or barbecue, then brush grill with oil. Grill chicken skewers until golden and tender, 2–3 minutes each side.

Steam or blanch choy sum in boiling water for about 2 minutes, until tender-crisp, then drain. Serve chicken warm with Mint Yogurt and choy sum.

To make Mint Yogurt: Combine yogurt, garlic, mint and cucumber. Mix until well combined. Cover and chill before serving.

Star anise chicken fillet with ginger risotto

Serves 4
4 chicken breast fillets, with skin
4 tablespoons vegetable oil
1 tablespoon rice wine
1 tablespoon soy sauce
1 tablespoon honey
2 tablespoons freshly grated ginger
2 cloves garlic, finely chopped
2 whole star anise
FOR GINGER RISOTTO
2 whole star anise

5½ cups (44 fl oz/1.35 L) chicken
    stock
3 tablespoons olive oil
1 onion, chopped
1 clove garlic, finely chopped
2 teaspoons freshly grated ginger
1½ cups (10½ oz/330 g) arborio rice
¼ cup (⅓ oz/10 g) chopped fresh
    cilantro (coriander) leaves
sea salt and freshly ground black
    pepper to taste

To make chicken: Using a sharp knife, pierce the skin side of each chicken fillet
3–5 times. Place chicken in a shallow nonmetallic dish. In a bowl, combine
2 tablespoons oil, rice wine, soy sauce, honey, ginger, garlic and star anise,
and pour over chicken fillets. Cover dish with plastic wrap and refrigerate for
3 hours. Drain chicken, reserving marinade.

Preheat a grill pan or barbecue, then lightly brush grill with the remaining oil.
Grill chicken fillets until golden and tender, 4–5 minutes each side, brushing
with reserved marinade during cooking. Test chicken by piercing the thickest
part with a skewer; chicken is cooked if the juices run clear. Remove from grill.

To make Ginger Risotto: In a medium saucepan over high heat, combine star
anise and stock and bring to boil. Reduce heat to low and allow stock to simmer.
Add onion, garlic and ginger and cook, stirring, until onion softens, about
2 minutes. Add rice, cook for 1 minute, stirring constantly until rice is coated
with oil. Add 1 cup stock to the pan, stirring constantly. Reduce heat, and allow
to simmer gently while stirring. Gradually add the remaining stock, 1 cup at a
time, until the rice is al dente and creamy. Stir in cilantro and season with salt
and pepper.

To serve, spoon risotto onto serving plates and top with chicken. Serve warm.

Spicy grilled chicken kibbeh

Serves 6
24 small bamboo skewers
2 oz (60 g) fine burghul (cracked wheat)
12 oz (375 g) chicken thigh fillets, coarsely chopped
½ teaspoon ground all spice
¼ teaspoon ground cayenne pepper
1 teaspoon ground cumin
½ teaspoon sea salt
½ teaspoon freshly ground black pepper
½ onion, coarsely chopped
½ cup (¾ oz/20 g) well packed mint leaves, finely chopped
2 tablespoons vegetable oil
lemon wedges, for serving
FOR DIPPING SAUCE
2 tablespoons olive oil
¼ cup (2 fl oz/60 ml) lemon juice
½ teaspoon cracked black pepper

Soak bamboo skewers in water for 10 minutes, then drain. Place burghul into a bowl and cover with cold water. Allow to stand 10 minutes, then drain. Squeeze out excess liquid using your hands. In a food processor, combine chicken, all spice, cayenne pepper, cumin, salt, pepper and onion and process until finely minced, about 30 seconds. Transfer mixture to a bowl, add burghul and mint, and mix until well combined. Divide into 24 portions. Shape each portion into a log shape and insert a skewer into each.

Preheat a grill pan or barbecue, then lightly brush grill with oil. Grill skewers until kibbeh is golden and tender, about 3–4 minutes. Remove from grill and serve warm with Dipping Sauce and lemon wedges.

To make Dipping Sauce: Combine olive oil, lemon juice and pepper and chill before serving.

Barbecue soy chicken

Serves 4

4 young chickens (spatchcocks), about 1 lb (500 g) each
⅓ cup (3 fl oz/90 ml) soy sauce
1 teaspoon sugar
3 tablespoons mirin
4 tablespoons olive oil
1 tablespoon grated ginger
2 cups (2 oz/60 g) salad greens such as watercress
and snowpea shoots, for serving

This recipe is best suited to an outdoor barbecue. Clean chickens and pat dry with paper towel. Truss chicken wings and legs securely with wetted string and place chickens in a shallow nonmetallic dish. In a bowl. combine soy sauce, sugar, mirin, 2 tablespoons olive oil and ginger and brush over chicken skin. Cover dish with plastic wrap and refrigerate for 1 hour. Drain, reserving marinade.

Preheat a barbecue, then brush lightly with the remaining oil. Grill chickens until golden and tender, 15–20 minutes, brushing with reserved marinade and turning chickens during cooking. Test chicken by piercing the thickest part with a skewer; chicken is cooked if the juices run clear. Remove from heat and serve hot or cold with salad greens.

Grilled chicken fillet with eggplant

Serves 4

4 chicken breast fillets

4 scallions (shallots/spring onions), coarsely chopped

4 cloves garlic

1 tablespoon chopped basil leaves

1 tablespoon chopped fresh cilantro (coriander) leaves

1/3 cup (3 fl oz/90 ml) soy sauce

1 teaspoon five spice powder

2 tablespoons mirin

1 tablespoon fish sauce

1 teaspoon sesame oil

1 tablespoon rice wine

2 teaspoons sugar

2 tablespoons vegetable oil

6 small thin eggplants (aubergines), sliced lengthwise into 1/16-inch (2-mm) slices

2 cups (2 oz/60 g) mizuna leaves, rinsed

Place the chicken in a shallow nonmetallic dish. In a food processor, combine scallions, garlic, basil, cilantro, soy sauce, five spice powder, mirin, fish sauce, sesame oil, rice wine and sugar and process until well blended, about 30 seconds. Pour marinade over chicken fillets, cover dish with plastic wrap and refrigerate for 2 hours. Drain chicken, reserving marinade.

Preheat a grill pan or barbecue, then brush grill lightly with vegetable oil. Grill chicken fillets until golden and tender, 4–5 minutes each side, brushing with reserved marinade during cooking. Test chicken by piercing the thickest part with a skewer; chicken is cooked if the juices run clear.

Remove from grill. Lightly brush eggplant slices with oil and grill until golden and tender, 1–2 minutes each side.

Place reserved marinade into a small saucepan, stir over medium heat and bring to a boil; allow to boil for 1 minute, then set aside.

To serve, arrange mizuna leaves on serving plates, top with eggplant then a chicken fillet. Drizzle with warm marinade.

Five spice grilled chicken

Serves 4

2 young chickens (spatchcocks), about
   1 lb (500 g) each
1 teaspoon sesame oil
1 tablespoon rice wine
4 tablespoons peanut oil
1 teaspoon five spice powder

1 teaspoon grated ginger
1 clove garlic, finely chopped
1 tablespoon honey
2 tablespoons soy sauce
1 red (Spanish) onion, cut into 8
   wedges
1 bunch choy sum, about 1 lb (500 g)

Clean chickens and pat dry with paper towel. Using poultry shears, cut in half through backbones and breastbones and place the pieces in a shallow nonmetallic dish.

In a bowl, combine sesame oil, rice wine, 2 tablespoons peanut oil, five spice powder, ginger, garlic, honey and soy sauce and mix until well combined. Brush mixture over chicken, then cover dish with plastic wrap. Refrigerate for 3 hours. Drain chicken, reserving marinade.

Preheat a barbecue, then lightly brush grill with the remaining peanut oil. Grill chicken halves until golden and tender, about 8 minutes each side, brushing with reserved marinade during cooking. Test chicken by piercing the thickest part with a skewer; chicken is cooked if the juices run clear. Remove from barbecue. Grill onion wedges until lightly browned, 1–2 minutes. Steam or blanch choy sum in boiling water until tender-crisp, about 2 minutes; then drain.

To serve, place choy sum onto serving plates, top with a chicken half, and garnish with red onion wedges.

HINT This recipe best suits an outdoor barbecue. If using an indoor grill pan, grill chicken halves until golden, then bake in a preheated 350°F (180°C/Gas 4) oven for 10–15 minutes to cook through. Otherwise substitute chicken halves for chicken breast fillets.

Fish and Seafood

Barbecued salmon
with wasabi butter

Serves 4
½ cup (4 oz/125 g) butter, softened
2 teaspoons wasabi paste
grated rind of 1 lime
1 tablespoon lime juice
½ teaspoon freshly ground black pepper
4 salmon fillets, approximately 6 oz/180 g each, skin and bones removed
2 tablespoons vegetable oil
fresh cilantro (coriander) leaves, for garnish
FOR CRISPY FRIED POTATOES
3 potatoes, peeled and very thinly sliced
½ cup (4 fl oz/125 ml) vegetable oil, for frying

In a mixing bowl, beat butter until soft. Add wasabi, rind, juice and pepper and mix until well combined. Refrigerate until firm. Brush salmon with oil. Preheat a grill pan or barbecue. Grill salmon 2–3 minutes each side (salmon should remain pink in the center), then allow to stand 5 minutes before cutting in half. Place onto serving plates. Using a teaspoon or melon baller, scoop wasabi butter onto salmon pieces. Serve with Crispy Fried Potatoes and garnish with fresh cilantro.

To make Crispy Fried Potatoes: Pat potato dry with paper towel. In a frying pan, heat oil over medium heat and, working in batches, fry potato slices until golden and crisp, about 2 minutes. Remove with a slotted spoon and drain on paper towel.

Spicy marinated tuna

Serves 4

4 fresh tuna steaks, approximately 6 oz (180 g) each
2 tablespoons soy sauce
⅓ cup (3 fl oz/90 ml) mirin
1 tablespoon sesame oil
1 teaspoon cracked black pepper
1 teaspoon ground cumin
1 teaspoon five spice powder
1 teaspoon sugar
1 teaspoon sea salt
1½ cups (1½ oz/45 g) mizuna leaves
lime wedges, for serving

Place tuna into a shallow nonmetallic dish. In a bowl, combine soy sauce, mirin and sesame oil, and brush over tuna. Cover dish with plastic wrap and refrigerate for 30 minutes. Drain, reserving marinade.

In a bowl, combine pepper, cumin, five spice powder, sugar and salt, and mix well. Sprinkle spice mix over tuna steaks. Preheat a grill pan or barbecue. Grill tuna, allowing it to remain pink in the center, 3–4 minutes each side. Remove from grill and allow to stand for 3 minutes.

In a small saucepan over medium heat, place reserved marinade and bring to a boil; boil for 1 minute, then set aside. Cut each tuna steak into wedges, arrange on serving plates and drizzle with warm marinade. Serve with mizuna leaves and lime wedges.

Mixed seafood skewers

Serves 4

12 bamboo skewers

8 oz (250 g) jumbo shrimp (king prawns), peeled and deveined, leaving tails intact

8 oz (250 g) scallops, cleaned

12 oz (375 g) white fish fillets, cut into 1½-inch (4-cm) cubes

4 tablespoons peanut oil, divided in half

½ onion, coarsely chopped

2 cloves garlic

2 teaspoons grated ginger

2 stems lemongrass (white section only), chopped

1 teaspoon shrimp paste

4 tablespoons soy sauce

1 teaspoon chili oil

1 teaspoon sesame oil

1 cup (1 oz/30 g) mizuna leaves, for serving

Soak bamboo skewers in cold water for 10 minutes, then drain. Pat shrimp, scallops and fish dry with paper towel and thread alternately onto skewers. Brush seafood skewers with 2 tablespoons peanut oil, then place into a shallow nonmetallic dish.

In a food processor, combine onion, garlic, ginger, lemongrass, shrimp paste, the remaining peanut oil, 1 tablespoon soy sauce, chili oil and sesame oil and

process until mixture becomes a smooth paste, about 30 seconds. Brush seafood with spice paste, then cover dish with plastic wrap and refrigerate for 30 minutes.

Preheat a grill pan or barbecue. Grill seafood skewers until seafood changes color, 3–4 minutes each side. Remove from grill. Serve warm with remaining soy sauce as a dipping sauce and mizuna leaves.

Fresh salmon cakes

Serves 4

2 tablespoons vegetable oil
1 lb (500 g) boneless and skinless salmon fillets
2 lb (1 kg) potatoes, peeled and chopped
3 tablespoons chopped dill
2 small red chili peppers, seeded and chopped
3 teaspoons freshly grated ginger
grated rind of 1 lime
1 teaspoon sea salt
½ teaspoon freshly ground pepper
½ cup (2½ oz/75 g) plain flour
2 eggs, beaten
2 tablespoons milk
3 cups (6 oz/180 g) fresh white breadcrumbs

Preheat a grill pan or barbecue, then brush grill with 1 tablespoon oil. Grill salmon until fish flakes easily when tested with a fork, 3–4 minutes each side (salmon should be cooked completely through). Remove from grill and allow to cool. In a saucepan of boiling water, cook potatoes until tender, about 8 minutes, then drain and mash. Allow to cool, about 10 minutes. Add salmon, dill, chili peppers, ginger, rind, salt and pepper. Using wet hands, mix thoroughly. Cover with plastic wrap and refrigerate for 1 hour. Divide into 12 portions and shape them into patties. Coat each patty in flour, dip into combined egg and milk, then coat in breadcrumbs.

Preheat a grill pan or barbecue and carefully brush grill with remaining oil. Cook salmon cakes until golden, 2–3 minutes each side. Remove from grill and serve warm or chilled with Green Aioli.

Green aioli

6 scallions (shallots/spring onions),
  coarsely chopped
¼ cup (⅓ oz/10 g) chopped basil
  leaves
3 cloves garlic, chopped
3 egg yolks
2 tablespoons lemon juice
¾ cup (6 fl oz/180 ml) virgin olive oil
sea salt and freshly ground black
  pepper

In a food processor, combine scallions, basil, garlic, egg yolks and lemon juice. Process until smooth, about 30 seconds. Gradually add olive oil while food processor motor is running and process until the mixture becomes a thick sauce. Season with salt and pepper to taste.

Shrimp, lime and chili pepper skewers

Serves 3–4
12 bamboo skewers
12 jumbo shrimp (king prawns), peeled, deveined, leaving tails intact
4 tablespoons vegetable oil
3 tablespoons lime juice
2 teaspoons grated ginger
2 cloves garlic, finely chopped
2 limes, cut into 6 wedges each
12 small red chili peppers
2 red (Spanish) onions, cut into 6 wedges each
1½ cups (1½ oz/45 g) mixed salad greens, for serving

Soak bamboo skewers in cold water for 10 minutes, then drain. Place shrimp in a shallow nonmetallic dish. In a small bowl, combine 2 tablespoons oil, juice, ginger and garlic, mix well and pour over shrimp. Cover dish with plastic wrap and refrigerate for 1 hour. Remove shrimp from marinade. Thread a shrimp, lime wedge, chili pepper and red onion wedge onto each skewer.

Preheat a grill pan or barbecue, then brush grill with the remaining oil. Grill skewers until shrimp change color, 2–3 minutes each side. Remove from grill and serve warm with salad greens.

Fish cutlet with sake

Serves 4
**4 fish steaks (cutlets), approximately 6½ oz (200 g) each
(choose any fish with firm, white flesh, such as sea bass,
grouper, halibut, coley or blue-eye cod)
2 teaspoons sea salt
1 teaspoon freshly ground black pepper
2 tablespoons vegetable oil
1 fl oz (30 ml) sake
juice and grated rind of 1 lime
2 cups (2 oz/60 g) baby spinach leaves, for serving
2 tablespoons additional grated lime rind, for serving**

Sprinkle both sides of fish with salt and pepper. Preheat a grill pan or barbecue, then brush grill with oil. Grill fish until fish changes color and flakes easily with a fork, 2–3 minutes each side. Remove from grill and brush each with combined sake, juice and rind.

To serve, arrange spinach leaves on serving plates and top with fish cutlets. Serve with extra lime rind.

Chili pepper, salt and pepper calamari

Serves 2–4
2 small red chili peppers, seeded and finely chopped
1 tablespoon sea salt
1 teaspoon cracked black pepper
16 baby squid (calamari), about 2 lb (1 kg), cleaned and halved
2 tablespoons vegetable oil
1½ cups (1½ oz/45 g) mizuna

Combine chili pepper, salt and pepper. Brush squid pieces with oil and press chili pepper mix into both sides of squid. Preheat a grill pan or barbecue. Grill squid pieces for 15–30 seconds each side. Remove from grill and serve on a bed of mizuna leaves.

Beef, Pork and Lamb

Grilled steak with
chili pepper and basil butter

Serves 4

4 oz (125 g) butter, softened
2 tablespoons chopped fresh cilantro (coriander) leaves
2 tablespoons chopped basil leaves
2 teaspoons grated lime rind
1 small red chili pepper, seeded and chopped
½ teaspoon freshly ground black pepper
4 tenderloin (scotch fillet or fillet) steaks, about 6½ oz (200 g) each
1 tablespoon olive oil
5 teaspoons chili oil

In a mixing bowl, beat butter until soft. Add cilantro, basil, lime rind, chili pepper and pepper, and mix until well combined. Spoon onto a piece of plastic wrap, roll into a log shape and refrigerate until firm, about 15 minutes.

Brush steaks with combined olive oil and 1 teaspoon chili oil. Preheat a grill pan or barbecue. Grill steaks until cooked to your liking, 2–3 minutes each side. Remove from grill and place onto serving plates.

Slice butter into ¼-inch (6-mm) rounds and place onto hot steaks. Serve with remaining chili oil for dipping.

HINT When cooking meat, avoid turning too frequently. Turning once halfway through the cooking time is usually sufficient. After cooking, cover meat with aluminium foil and let rest for 10 minutes to enhance the flavor.

Pork and apple skewers

Serves 6–8
24 bamboo skewers
1 lb (500 g) pork tenderloin (fillets), cut into 1½-inch (4-cm) cubes
2 red apples, cut into 12 wedges each
5 tablespoons vegetable oil
2 tablespoons lime juice
1 tablespoon soy sauce
2 tablespoons chopped fresh cilantro (coriander) leaves
2 kaffir lime leaves, finely shredded
1 tablespoon chopped Thai basil
1 teaspoon sea salt
1 teaspoon freshly ground black pepper
1 clove garlic, finely chopped

Soak skewers in cold water for 10 minutes, then drain. Place pork and apple wedges onto skewers and place in a shallow nonmetallic dish. In a bowl, combine 3 tablespoons oil, juice, soy sauce, cilantro, lime leaves, basil, salt, pepper and garlic, and mix well. Brush over pork and apple, cover dish with plastic wrap and refrigerate for 30 minutes. Drain off marinade.

Preheat a grill pan or barbecue, then brush grill with remaining oil. Grill skewers until pork is tender, 2–3 minutes per side. Remove from grill and serve warm.

Soy beef skewers

Serves 3–4
12 bamboo skewers
8 oz (250 g) sirloin (rump) steak
5 tablespoons soy sauce
2 tablespoons oyster sauce
1 teaspoon sugar
2 tablespoons mirin
2 teaspoons sesame oil
1 clove garlic, finely chopped
1 tablespoon chopped fresh cilantro (coriander) leaves
2 tablespoons vegetable oil

Soak skewers in cold water for
10 minutes, then drain. Slice steak
into thin long strips, about 1 inch by
4 inches (2.5 cm by 10 cm). Thread
strips onto skewers and place in a
shallow nonmetallic dish. In a bowl,
combine 2 tablespoons soy sauce,
oyster sauce, sugar, mirin, sesame oil,
garlic and coriander, and mix well.
Brush marinade over beef, cover with
plastic wrap and refrigerate for
30 minutes. Drain off marinade.

Preheat a grill pan or barbecue,
then brush grill with oil. Grill beef
skewers until tender, 2–3 minutes.
Remove from grill and serve hot with
remaining soy sauce as a dipping
sauce.

Barbecued rack of lamb

Serves 6–8
3 fl oz (90 ml) lime juice
3 fl oz (90 ml) olive oil
3 tablespoons chopped fresh cilantro (coriander) leaves
5 cloves garlic, finely chopped
2 teaspoons sea salt
1 teaspoon freshly ground black pepper
3 teaspoons ground cumin
1 teaspoon ground coriander
2 racks of lamb, 8 cutlets each, excess fat trimmed
2 tablespoons additional olive oil
4 limes, cut in half
3 tablespoons Chili Jam, for serving

In a bowl, combine juice, olive oil, cilantro, garlic, salt, pepper, cumin and coriander, and mix until well combined. Place lamb in a shallow nonmetallic dish and brush with herb mixture. Cover dish with plastic wrap and refrigerate for 3–4 hours. Remove lamb from marinade.

Preheat a grill pan or barbecue, then brush grill with 2 tablespoons oil. Grill lamb until just pink in the center when cut, about 8 minutes each side. Remove from heat, cover with aluminum foil and allow to stand for 5 minutes. Grill lime halves until lightly golden, 1–2 minutes. Slice lamb racks into 2 cutlet sections and serve warm with lime halves and Chili Jam.

HINT This recipe is best suited to an outdoor barbecue.

Chili jam

Makes ½ cup (4 fl oz/125 ml)

10 dried chili peppers
⅓ cup (3 fl oz/90 ml) peanut oil
1 red bell pepper (capsicum), seeded,
**   deribbed and chopped**
cloves from 1 head of garlic, coarsely
**   chopped**
6 oz (185 g) shallots (French shallots),
**   chopped**
½ cup (3 oz/90 g) shaved palm sugar
**   or packed brown sugar**
2 tablespoons tamarind paste

Put chili peppers in a bowl and add boiling water to cover. Let stand for 15 minutes, or until softened. Drain, seed and chop chilies. In a food processor, combine chilies, oil, bell pepper, garlic and shallots. Blend until smooth, about 30 seconds.

In a wok or skillet over medium heat, cook chili mixture, stirring constantly, for 15 minutes. Add sugar and tamarind. Reduce heat to low and simmer, until mixture darkens and thickens to a jam-like consistency, about 10 minutes.

Store in a sterilized jar in the refrigerator for up to 3 months.

Chili beef burgers

Serves 4

1 lb (500 g) ground (minced) lean beef

1 clove garlic, crushed

1 small red chili pepper, seeded and finely chopped

1 small yellow (brown) onion, grated

2 tablespoons chopped fresh cilantro (coriander)

1 tablespoon vegetable oil, for brushing

4 cups (4 oz/125 g) arugula (rocket)

20 Vietnamese mint leaves

½ cup (¾ oz/20 g) loosely packed fresh cilantro (coriander) leaves

1 tablespoon chili oil

salt and freshly ground black pepper

4 crusty rolls, halved

¼ cup (2 fl oz/60 ml) Thai sweet chili sauce, optional

In a bowl, combine beef, garlic, chili pepper, onion and chopped cilantro. Using wet hands, mix well. Divide into 4 portions and shape each portion into a patty, flattening it slightly to fit size of roll.

Brush both sides of beef patties with vegetable oil and on a preheated barbecue or grill pan, grill until cooked through to center, 3–4 minutes per side.

In a bowl, combine arugula, mint and cilantro. Drizzle with chili oil and season with salt and pepper. Place greens on bottom halves of rolls. Add beef patties and drizzle with Thai sweet chili sauce if desired. Add tops of rolls and serve.

Beef tenderloin with papaya relish

Serves 4–6

1½ lb (750 g) piece whole beef
tenderloin (fillet)

2 teaspoons chili oil

3 tablespoons chopped basil leaves

2 tablespoons chopped fresh cilantro
(coriander) leaves

4 tablespoons vegetable oil

6 thin slices prosciutto (Italian ham)

FOR PAPAYA RELISH

½ small fresh papaya, skin removed,
seeded and chopped

4 scallions (shallots/spring onions),
sliced

2 tablespoons chopped basil leaves

2 tablespoons chopped fresh cilantro
(coriander) leaves

3 fl oz (90 ml) Thai sweet chili sauce

Truss beef with string to hold in shape and place in a shallow nonmetallic dish. In a bowl, combine chili oil, basil, cilantro and 2 tablespoons vegetable oil and mix well. Spread mixture over meat, cover dish with plastic wrap and refrigerate for at least 1 hour.

Meanwhile, grill or pan-fry prosciutto until golden and crisp. Remove and drain on paper towel. Allow to cool, then break each in half and set aside.

Preheat a barbecue, then brush grill with remaining vegetable oil. Grill beef for 12–15 minutes, turning during cooking. Remove from grill, wrap in aluminum foil and allow to stand for 10 minutes, then cut into 4 thick steaks.

To make Papaya Relish: In a bowl, combine papaya, scallions, basil, cilantro and chili sauce, and mix well. Refrigerate until serving.

To serve, place crisp prosciutto pieces onto serving plates, top with beef steak and spoon Papaya Relish over beef. Serve immediately.

Barbecued lamb cutlets

Serves 6
1-inch (2.5-cm) cinnamon stick
1 teaspoon black peppercorns
1 teaspoon finely grated fresh ginger
1 teaspoon crushed garlic
6 fresh green chili peppers, crushed to a paste
½ teaspoon salt
2 lb (1 kg) lamb cutlets
vegetable oil, for brushing
2 red (Spanish) or yellow (brown) onions, thinly sliced into rings, for serving
1 cup (1 oz/30 g) fresh mint leaves, for serving

In a spice grinder, grind cinnamon and peppercorns to a powder. Place in a bowl and combine with ginger, garlic, chili pepper and salt. Rub mixture over both sides of lamb cutlets and set aside to marinate for at least 30 minutes.

When hot, brush oil over barbecue plate and place cutlets on top. Cook lamb, brushing with oil when necessary, until cooked to your liking, 3–4 minutes per side.

Serve hot, topped with onion rings and mint leaves and accompanied with lemon wedges and Mint Yogurt (see page 25 for Mint Yogurt recipe).

HINT This recipe is best suited to an outdoor barbecue.

Vegetables

Tofu and scallion satays

Serves 3–4

12 bamboo skewers

12 oz (375 g) firm tofu, cut into
   1¼-inch (3-cm) cubes

8 scallions (shallots/spring onions), cut
   into 2-inch (5-cm) lengths

2 tablespoons soy sauce

1 teaspoon sesame oil

1 clove garlic, finely chopped

2 tablespoons vegetable oil

FOR SATAY SAUCE

3 tablespoons smooth peanut butter

4 cloves garlic, chopped

1 teaspoon chili oil

2 tablespoons soy sauce

pinch sea salt

2 teaspoons sugar

2 tablespoons hot water

1 tablespoon hot bean paste

Soak skewers in cold water for 10 minutes, then drain. Place tofu and scallion lengths alternately onto bamboo skewers and place skewers in a shallow dish. In a bowl, combine soy sauce, sesame oil and garlic, and brush over tofu and scallions. Cover dish with plastic wrap and refrigerate for 30 minutes. Drain off marinade.

Preheat a grill pan or barbecue, then brush grill with vegetable oil. Grill tofu and scallion skewers until golden, 1–2 minutes each side. Remove from grill and serve warm with Satay Sauce.

To make Satay Sauce: In a food processor, combine peanut butter, garlic, chili oil, soy sauce, salt, sugar, hot water and hot bean paste. Process until smooth.

HINT Leftover Satay Sauce can be stored in a screw-top jar in the refrigerator for up to 7 days.

Potato and rosemary skewers

Serves 3–4

12 long woody stems of fresh rosemary

1½ lb (750 g) sweet potatoes

12 small baby potatoes (chats)

2 tablespoons vegetable oil

1 teaspoon chili oil

1 teaspoon dried thyme leaves

2 cloves garlic, finely chopped

1 teaspoon sea salt

¼ teaspoon freshly ground black pepper

⅓ cup (3 fl oz/90 ml) Thai sweet chili sauce, for dipping

Trim rosemary stems to 6 inch (15 cm) lengths and remove the leaves 4 inches (10 cm) from base of stem. Soak stems in cold water for 30 minutes, then drain.

Peel sweet potatoes and cut into 1½ inch (4 cm) cubes. In a large saucepan of salted water, cook sweet potato cubes and baby potatoes until tender when pierced with a skewer, 8–10 minutes. Drain and refresh under cold running water. Pat vegetables dry with paper towel and cut each baby potato in half.

Thread potatoes carefully onto rosemary stems and place in a shallow dish. In a bowl, combine oils, thyme leaves, garlic, salt and pepper, and brush over potatoes. Cover dish with plastic wrap and stand for 30 minutes. Preheat a grill pan or barbecue, then grill potato and rosemary skewers until golden, 1–2 minutes each side. Remove from grill and serve hot with Thai sweet chili sauce as a dipping sauce.

Tofu and vegetable timbales with lemon spinach sauce

Makes 4

5 oz (150 g) firm tofu, drained
⅓ cup (3 fl oz/90 ml) balsamic vinegar
¼ cup (2 fl oz/60 ml) olive oil
1 red bell pepper (capsicum), seeded and quartered
3 baby Japanese long eggplants (aubergines), thinly sliced crosswise
2 medium zucchini, thinly sliced crosswise

1 small sweet potato, peeled and thinly sliced crosswise

FOR LEMON SPINACH SAUCE
4 cups (4 oz/125 g) baby spinach leaves
2 tablespoons fresh lemon juice
1 clove garlic, finely chopped
3 tablespoons olive oil

Cut tofu into ½ inch (12 mm) thick slices and marinate in 2 tablespoons of balsamic vinegar for 15 minutes. Drain and pat dry with paper towels.

In a bowl, combine olive oil and remaining vinegar. Brush vegetables with oil mixture. Grill tofu and vegetables until lightly browned, 2–3 minutes on each side for tofu and 3–4 minutes on each side for vegetables.

Lightly grease four 6 fl oz (180 ml) ramekins and layer each with 1 slice of eggplant, 1 piece of tofu, 1 teaspoon of Lemon Spinach Sauce, 1 sweet potato slice, 1 bell pepper slice, 1 zucchini slice and another sweet potato slice. To serve, invert each timbale onto a small plate, swirl extra spinach sauce around timbale.

To make Lemon Spinach Sauce: In a food processor, combine spinach, lemon juice, garlic and oil and puree until smooth. Set aside

Grilled vegetables with warm ginger dressing

Serves 2–4
2 baby fennel, cut in half lengthwise
4 baby bok choy, cut in half lengthwise
4 small eggplants (aubergines), cut in half lengthwise
2 red (Spanish) onions, cut into 6 wedges each
2 long red chili peppers, cut in half lengthwise
12 fresh asparagus spears, trimmed
2 tablespoons vegetable oil
3 cloves garlic, finely chopped
FOR WARM GINGER DRESSING
3 teaspoons sesame oil
2 tablespoons vegetable oil
3 teaspoons freshly grated ginger
⅓ cup (3 fl oz/90 ml) lime juice
2 tablespoons mirin

Place prepared vegetables in a shallow dish. In a bowl, combine oil and garlic and toss through vegetables until well coated.

Preheat a grill pan or barbecue. Working in batches, grill vegetables until golden, 1–2 minutes each side. Remove from grill, place into serving bowls and drizzle with Warm Ginger Dressing. Serve immediately.

To make Warm Ginger Dressing: In a small saucepan, combine oils, ginger, lime juice and mirin. Whisk over a low heat until just warm, about 1 minute, and serve.

Glossary

ARBORIO RICE A type of short grain rice originally grown in Italy and traditionally used to make risotto. The high starch content of the grains gives risotto its characteristic creamy texture.

ARUGULA (ROCKET) An aromatic salad green with a peppery mustard flavor.

BOK CHOY A small Asian variety of cabbage with thick white stems and mild-flavored dark green leaves. If unavailable, use Chinese broccoli or choy sum.

CHILI OIL Spicy oil produced by steeping dried red chili peppers in oil. Use this hot oil only by the drop. Store in refrigerator after opening.

CHINESE FIVE SPICE Made from an equal mixture of ground Szechuan peppercorns, star anise, fennel, cloves and cinnamon. Available from most supermarkets.

CHOY SUM A Chinese green also known as flowering cabbage. It has yellow flowers, thin stems and a mild flavor, and is suitable in most recipes calling for Asian greens. The entire vegetable (stems, leaves and flowers) is used.

CRACKED WHEAT (BURGHUL) The whole wheat berry broken into coarse, medium or fine particles. Also called burghul. Popular in Middle Eastern cooking.

GINGER Gnarled and bumpy root with a spicy, pungent odor and slightly sweet and peppery taste. Peel the paper-thin skin with the back of a knife before grating or chopping finely. Popular in Asian and Indian cooking.

HOT BEAN PASTE A hot, thick red-brown sauce made from fermented soybeans, chili peppers, garlic and spices. Sometimes called red bean or chili bean paste.

KAFFIR LIMES AND LIME LEAVES Leaves from the kaffir lime tree are used to add an enticing citrus flavor and aroma to dishes. The juice and rind of the fruit are also used in cooking. Regular lime juice and rind can be substituted.

FIRM TOFU An all-purpose tofu that holds its shape during cooking. Made from soybeans and creamy in texture. Available in refrigerated vacuum-sealed containers as well as shelf stable cartons that require no refrigeration until opened.

FISH SAUCE A pungent sauce of salted, fermented fish and other seasonings, used in sauces, dressings and dipping sauces. Fish sauce from Thailand, called nam pla, is commonly available. Don't be put off by the strong fishy smell; there is really no substitute.

LEMONGRASS A popular lemon-scented grass widely used in Thai cooking. Trim the root, discard top third and any tough outer layers, chopping finely or bruise (hitting with meat mallet or blunt side of a chef's knife) to infuse flavor.

MIRIN Sweet alcoholic wine made from rice and used in Japanese cooking. Sweet sherry can be substituted.

MIZUNA A feathery Japanese salad green with a delicate flavor. If unavailable, other varieties of salad greens can be substituted.

OYSTER SAUCE A thick, dark brown Chinese sauce made from fermented dried oysters and soy sauce and sold in bottles. Store in refrigerator after opening.

PALM SUGAR Dense, dark cakes of sugar made from the sap of palm trees. Thinly shave or grate before using. Substitute with brown sugar if unavailable.

RICE WINE Sweet, low-alcohol Chinese wine, also known as Shaoxing wine, made from glutinous rice. Sake or dry sherry can be used as a substitute.

SAKE A clear Japanese wine made from fermented rice.

SESAME OIL An intensely flavored oil made from sesame seeds, sold in bottles, and widely used in Asian cooking. There is no real substitute.

SHRIMP PASTE A pungent-flavored paste produced by drying, salting and pounding shrimp, then forming it into blocks or cakes.

SOY SAUCE A salty sauce made from fermented soybeans and usually wheat, and sold in bottles and cans. Available in light and dark varieties, the dark is usually used in cooking and the lighter soy for dipping sauces.

TAHINI A thick oily paste made from sesame seeds and traditionally used in Middle Eastern cooking.

TAMARIND PASTE Made from sour-sweet fruit of tropical tamarind tree. Sold in jars and tubes in Asian markets. If unavailable, substitute with fresh lime juice.

THAI BASIL Refers to several Asian basil varieties including holy, purple and sweet. Any basil can be used as a substitute.

THAI SWEET CHILI SAUCE A mild chili sauce with a sweet after-taste. Usually used as a dipping sauce, it can also be used on burgers and barbecued meats.

VIETNAMESE MINT LEAVES A spicy hot variety of mint that is delicious in salads. Substitute with regular mint if unavailable.

WASABI PASTE Hot, Japanese green horseradish, traditionally served with sushi and sashimi. Available as a paste in ready-to-use tubes or in a powdered form to be mixed with water.

Index

A LANSDOWNE BOOK

Published by Apple Press
Sheridan House
4th Floor
112-116 Western Road
Hove
East Sussex BN3 1DD UK

www.apple-press.com

Copyright © 2003 text, photography and design: Lansdowne Publishing Pty Ltd

Created and produced by Lansdowne Publishing
Text: Vicki Liley
Photographer: Louise Lister
Stylist: Vicki Liley
Designer: Avril Makula
Editor: Joanne Holliman
Production Manager: Sally Stokes
Project Co-ordinator: Kathleen Davidson

ISBN 1 84543 004 2

All rights reserved. No part of this publication may be reproduced, stored in
a retrieval system, or transmitted in any form, or by any means, electronic,
mechanical, photocopying, recording, or otherwise, without the prior written
permission of the publisher.

Set in Trade Gothic, Journal Text, Gill Sans and Neuropol on QuarkXPress
Printed in Singapore by Tien Wah Press

Cover picture: Whole beef tenderloin with papaya relish, page 51
Pictured on page 2: Barbecued rack of lamb, page 48
Pictured on page 4: Spicy marinated tuna, page 36

BARBECUE